I0158197

Three Songs
for
Children

Three Songs
for
Children

Poems

John Urban

Three Songs for Children
Copyright © 2017 by John Urban

All rights reserved. No part of this book may be reproduced in any form or by any electronic or mechanical means including information storage and retrieval systems, without permission in writing from the author.

Cover photo "Big Sur Dusk" by Ron Lampi — *www.ronlampi.com*

Book design by River Sanctuary Graphic Arts

ISBN 978-1-935914-72-3

Printed in the United States of America

Reminiscences appeared in the *Common Ground Review*, *2015 Summer Issue*

Contact author at:
johnurb@sbcglobal.net

Additional copies available from:
www.riversanctuarypublishing.com

RIVER SANCTUARY PUBLISHING
P.O. Box 1561
Felton, California 95018
www.riversanctuarypublishing.com
Dedicated to the awakening of the New Earth

Contents

Endings, Beginnings

I

Along and down a lighted road,
daylight's end, night's begun,
evening's tale is told.

II

Black Sam pulled a knife,
and the light from the lamp, I swear,
cracked off the window
and parted Albert's golden hair.

Max and Elinore

"The weather's changing," Elinore remarked,
looking upward out the window through a cool, grey light.

The light struck Max. He stepped to the window,
and glanced out. "You're right," he said.

In the Mountains

I

In the morning, when you rise,
Love is told—sunlight of your eyes
Smiles upon a dappled, wooded world.

II

A signature upon a stone o'erturned,
A ring of ash settling into loam,
Where, the night before, a campfire burned.

III

Under a blue, shell-like horn of a moon,
An ancient, lichen-spotted saddle-post
Crumbles into a yellowing meadow—an airy,
Ashen-faced sentinel who whispers, "El Dorado!"

At the Coast

The light comes in on wings
Over a flat, farm-checked valley floor.

Down a brown, earthen path,
Through the dew-sprinkled grass.

A hillside's blush of blue,
A tawny beach's graceful flanks.

To say life arose in the ocean
Is not to say life came from the ocean.

Wisps of coral-colored cloud.

Poseidon's Keep

Just beyond the ocean's salty reach
We walk—the bright, rumbling talk.

Deathlessly, the stepped breakers drop,
Then wash, one by one, onto the beach.

A distant ocean mimics the human reach;
A collected, watery being—a fiery thief.

The Old Woman

Old woman, I know the aging flesh you wear
And though body wither and drop, it is not
That face I see: God gives His ineffable mercy.

To each life, its purpose—you shoulder
Anew the fleshly garment and through
Its tangled light live the needed life.

Unencumbered, noble light now graciously
Wends her way, removes the ancient debt,
And her word is inscribed, once again, upon
Your thought-to-be-obliterated human step.

He Speaks

For J.R.

Thus we know the hour of release.
Be gentle, and now, therefore, go—
Old Death but a painted fear.

Spirit, arise! the dust is shaken;
Darkness dims no longer
These unlearned, these life-forsaken, eyes.

Dark Spring

Autumn bedecked in robes
Of shimmering, darkening leaves.

"Pure water," spake the ground;
Mother Beauty, " I " am pleased.

Three Songs for Children

I

The Heavenly Car

Its lustrous sheen, silky green,
It doth wash itself
With soapy stream and water.

II

The Wooden Bug

Dear Bug, dear Bug
Upon yon shimmering Tree,
Speak, speak,
Speak the Truth to me.

III

The Paper Cat

Little Tiger, do you pounce and bite?
More wise than Minnaloushe tonight.

O, but *you* only pretend—
Paper Tiger, tumble down again!

Night Gates

As evening comes, silence descends
Upon the house and the surrounding grounds.

Mother and father move easily about, secure
Within the bosom of such a great spirit as he.

Unsaid, but secretly and tacitly anticipated,
Are the even greater silences that will be imparted
As each member of the family tumbles into bed.

Along the Ridge

A silver-struck spire of a trunk
Bespeaks its ghostly message.

Fallen brothers, limbs broken
And scattered askew,
Meld with hillside and stone,
Embracing death's forgotten lots.

Loosely released, light-sustained,
The " I " streams partly past,
Brightly weaves beyond, the frozen,
Lifeless gates once locked to thought.

The rosy canyon floods with blood,
Accepts a sacrificial self—from altered ash
A deathless David spurns the cumbered earth,
Bursting upon an Orphic sky of song.

The Beneficents

We went to the land where the greatest ones
Who had ever lived had established their homes
And had their being. Before us lay the darkling port
With its sea of gold and its golden tributaries.

The kiss of light came from the islands and fell
Upon our brows—we stood within their forms,
Amidst workshops of unimaginable monument.

We saw the stone; the six-fingered daughters and sons;
The star-scarred old men; and, the immortals, who now
Gathered together, now dispersed, with their shell-like
Transparency and light, evening's endless battalions of cloud
Or its ragged, revolving fogs that marshal like stone
Against a darkening world's dark and western-most wood.

Dark Tower

But one, leaving the city, did not,
and crossing the desert, he reached the mountains
and the face he carved therein was his own.

And now, with his daughters, seeks
almighty night among the stars.

So, lift your eyes to the far, far future,
and there, in those vast and shifting puzzles of light,
stand poised your past, and passing, friends.

The Child and the Mirror

A child looks into a mirror
And able to see only himself,
First reaches out to those things
That are of himself; whereas,
We, who are a little older,
If we have been successful,
Inquire beyond ourselves, beyond
Our respective situations or fates.

The Cycles of Kathleen

I

You imagine you see me as I am, but,
In reality, you see me only as I appear.

Love goes beyond appearances
To that which is the essence.

It is your essence I seek, not your vision;
It is *you* I would hold, not your life.

II

The Searcher and the Sought For

The girl gave of her cup to drink
And I drank and myself I saw.

She held before me a mirror
And said, *"Is this whom ye seek?*

Behold, I am here. The chambers
Of your heart are graven in me; for thee
Was I made, in me is what you seek."

III

Motion sideways was impossible, so one
Clung to the stubborn spar of the ship
Praying the water wouldn't extinguish it
Like a flame—though later, piloted upon
The toothéd rocks, the ship splintered;
Fragments of oars spun heavenward
Amidst tackles of flying rope and foam,
But through the eruption our ship of stars.
The Unicorn and I had come home.

IV

The long-forgotten sails of wind
Tremble upon the shoreline's bend
Where, walking, Kathleen and I
Send glances of everlasting love.

Poetic Tales

I

We do not know what Poetry is,
We know only what it has been,
And we work only toward what it might be.

II

Leaving the leafy protection of the skies,
We hastened forward, bringing with us
What tales of our adventures we could.

III

Brightly down the colored gullies
The pebbles rolled, jostling
Till surfaces gleamed like gems.

IV

It is difficult to imagine the intrusion
Of elements that tell another tale,
But in the flat reaches of light
Voices speak that otherwise are still.

Reminiscences

Shelley, or the man Keats,
Which one he didn't remember,
But there was the Old Church
With its moldering stones.

As a child, he walked its paths
In the dry-twigged spring
And the earth exhaled its secrets.

The dead, being given duty,
Sent forth their forces—subtle
Fingers that troubled the buds.

Penitencia Creek

Sandra patiently toils among the rocks
Of Penitencia Creek, stooping now and then
To examine, myopically, her catch.

Wray, shortly before an ill-starred marriage,
Sits on the banks of the same creek, and watching
A white horse slowly descend the opposite slope
Into shadows and wood, now says he believes in God.

And here, years later, remembered faces and forms,
Philosophies, tangle and untangle their way
Along these basins of tumbled rock
Like the roots of the trees of the creek of Penitencia.

Dark Forest, Bright Forms

O shaggy Fathers, born of this fog-scudding night, does
At last the light from the habitations of men shine upon you?

And in some near-distant future, will that shining spell
Spell your end, the end to your somber-misted beauty?

A beauty of which our thought should partake, not
A meager repast of thin and desiccated argument.

Argument which pummels us down dwindling paths
To a dark and stony shore with its waiting skiff.

O shaggy Fathers, born of this fog-scudding night, to walk
Among your light and towering forms, to *feel* a tempered home!

A Small, Tendrilled Path

The small, tendrilled path came to the same place
As before, but I did not see she who had guided me.

Outside a small nearby hut, a huge parrot
Angelically rustled its feathers, then, like a slow,
Unfocused light, numbingly floated from his perch
To the porch where (after awkward steps) he fixed
An eye upon me, then, seemingly, upon another.

Stepping gently upon the weathered wooden porch
I peered past a door left ajar, but, still, no one was to be seen,
Although, I suddenly realized, here were the rooms
Where, if into whose depths I stepped, she was to be found.

www.ingramcontent.com/pod-product-compliance
Lightning Source LLC
Chambersburg PA
CBHW021920040426
42448CB00007B/837